WEIGHTLIFTING FOR BEGINNERS

The best plan to building muscle
rapidly, safely and healthily for
a long term strong body

Nathan Paradise

ISBN-13: 9798797449690

Cover design by: Art Painter
Library of Congress Control Number: 2018675309
Printed in the United States of America

Safety Disclaimer
The advice provided in this book is not medical advice. Anyone starting
weight training should be appropriately fit to do so. Please consult your doc-
tor or physician before undergoing training under weight, especially if you
have underlying health issues. Please stay safe and be careful when working
with weights. The writer of the book does not take any liability for injuries
or diseases potentially caused in the reader's training, diet or lifestyle.

CONTENTS

Title Page

Copyright

Weightlifting for Beginners   1

Introduction   3

Chapter 1: Hypertrophy - the Key to Building Muscle   5

What is Hypertrophy?   7

How Many Repetitions to Gain Muscle?   9

How to Maximize Hypertrophy to Build Muscle as Quick as   12
Possible

The Different Methods to Maximize Building Muscles   15

Chapter 2: Strength Equals Hypertrophy and Hypertrophy   17
Equals Strength?

Chapter 3: Technique is Key   21

Basic Weight Training Safety Techniques   24

Chapter 4: The Rules to Follow - getting started   29

Types of Muscle Contractions: Concentric, Eccentric and   33
Isometric

Concentric Contraction

The Eccentric Contraction

Isometric Contraction

Plyometric Contraction

Chapter 5: Weightlifting Steps: 39

Weightlifting Warming Exercises   41

The Six Core Movements   44

More Advanced Moves   50

Additional Exercises   52

Chapter 6: Weightlifting and Diet   57

Main Macronutrients Needed for Hypertrophy   60

Supplements   64

Chapter 7: The Importance of a Plan   67

Hypertrophy Final Tips   74

CONCLUSION   77

Bonuses   79

WEIGHTLIFTING FOR BEGINNERS

Dedicated To Beginners Into Weightlifting

Don't be afraid of being a beginner into weightlifting, because some are born strong, and others become strong through. This book is dedicated to those who think they will never succeed in building muscles and weightlifting. This book has been written with the objective of making your weightlifting experience a pleasant one.

INTRODUCTION

Millions of people go to fitness centers to get into shape and get the perfect body they are looking for. They want to sculpt their body, build muscle or gain strength naturally, without using doping products. But the existing books and methods they find are often outdated; which does not allow progress to be made beyond a certain threshold and does not adapt to the physical characteristics of each person.

What are the basics to know before starting? What are the essential techniques to progress, the workouts to favor to build up muscle or even the nutritional information essential to eat well or supplement? Indeed, on this framework, we offer you this weightlifting book which helps innovate weightlifting with a revolutionary training strategy and techniques in bodybuilding based both on the most recent studies in sports science and on an extraordinary experience, and based on various effective techniques.

This book for weightlifting and bodybuilding will be for the first time your detailed resource, destined to become your only trusted guide to weight lifting. Weightlifting is about one major physical factor, strength. In order to improve this factor, specific training is carried out. One book, many possibilities, this book has been designed to satisfy each reader, whatever their objective and starting point in weightlifting.

This book describes in a clear and precise way most of the bodybuilding movements. I will carry to you all the practical information that you need to learn how to weightlift to allow the beginner or the professional athlete to build muscles in a short time.

Everything is here in this book and what makes this guide so strong is that it really contains all the important information to achieve the goals you have set for yourself, whether you want to improve your strength, sculpt your figure or lose mass. Whether you are a beginner athlete or not, it doesn't matter. If you want to avoid multiplying the number of books to read and want a complete one that covers just about every topic, this guide is definitely the one I would recommend.

Because in the majority of sports, strength training is essential, weightlifting is also indispensable. This is a strength training program that can bring about beneficial and positive changes in the body, internally and externally. So what are these changes? How to describe the benefits of strength training on the body? This book offers you an overview of weightlifting in addition to the following points:
- Hypertrophy - what is it and why is it the key to building muscle?
- Strength equals hypertrophy and hypertrophy equals strength?
- Weightlifting techniques
- Beginner friendly exercises
- The 6 core movements
- More advanced moves
- Additional exercises
- Weightlifting and diet
- A plan
- Final weightlifting tips

CHAPTER 1: HYPERTROPHY - THE KEY TO BUILDING MUSCLE

There are many reasons for training. Being in good health or having a strong physical condition is definitely ahead of the pack. For some, having a good body mass index (BMI) will be the benchmark. For others, physical appearance will be on top of the list. It may come as a surprise, but regardless of the source of motivation, the goal, muscle hypertrophy is a practice that meets almost all cases.

Whether aesthetics, weight gain, performance, the reasons for better understanding muscle hypertrophy is key. It is through the detailed understanding of the latter that you can then choose the program most suited to your needs. Understanding muscle hypertrophy is one of the major issues in bodybuilding and physical preparation for weightlifting. Thus, even before being able to claim to improve its maximum strength and its nervous qualities, or generate more tension in the muscle by weight or speed, it is necessary to understand what hypertrophy is.

To better understand muscle hypertrophy, let's start with a definition. Muscle hypertrophy can be defined as an increase in the overall size of muscle tissue - basically muscle growth. Growth occurs by adding sarcomeres (a scientific unit for measuring muscle fibers). We can often associate hypertrophy with substantial muscle mass gain, it is often seen as an approach reserved for bodybuilders. Misunderstood, it is nevertheless very useful. One of the goals often expressed is the desire to firm and tone the body. It basically represents hypertrophy.

This chapter will therefore take stock of what hypertrophy actually is. I will highlight the benefits associated with the method while breaking down some preconceptions. An overview of the ways to achieve the desired results will complete the picture of hypertrophy.

WHAT IS HYPERTROPHY?

In addition to an aesthetic goal, having a certain muscle mass is a basic component of optimal physical condition. We should all want a base of mass, good muscle tone, and for a few, some definition.

Hypertrophy training encompasses all of these goals well and even prevents certain physical problems that arise with age.

Indeed, after the age 30 years old, we trend to lose 3-5% of our muscle mass each year by remaining inactive. This phenomenon is called sarcopenia. However, staying active can slow this process down.

You can probably guess where I'm going with this. Since the main goal of hypertrophy training is to increase muscle mass, we fight sarcopenia. Resistance training with weights and more specifically, strength training (with a certain load) will be the most useful tools in this context.

Let me take a break from strength training. A preconceived idea we have of this type of training has to lift excessively heavy loads. Strength training does not automatically equal lifting 300 lbs. It is a workout that will cause you to lift heavier and heavier loads depending on your level of physical condition.

The goal of strength training is to gradually increase the loads each week or, sometimes, each workout. As it will be appropriate to lift "heavy", a reduced number of repetitions for a movement (typically 6-15 or less) will be effective. This will result in a shorter but more demanding effort.

HOW MANY REPETITIONS TO GAIN MUSCLE?

Are you wondering how many reps per set do you need to perform to gain muscle mass? Do you want long, medium or short sets? Each approach has been touted as an ideal way to build muscle. Some people argue passionately for either approach, but compelling conclusions are rare. Thus, we are going to separate each case, from long sets, through medium sets, to short sets. This will help you reach a verdict on the right choice to make in order to increase muscle mass.

1 - Long series (15 repetitions or more)
The sets of more than 15 reps have one drawback: the amount of weight you can lift is not heavy enough to recruit your fast, type 2 muscle fibers. Put simply, type 2 fibers are where the potential for muscle growth resides, and they only respond to heavy loads, those that are at least 75% of the maximum weight lifted on a repetition.

Long sets are, however, a great way to increase muscle endurance and training volume at the end of your workout, when you're out of strength. If you're looking for a specific improvement for playing a sport, especially sports like endurance running, long sets can help. But, if muscle bulk, and especially strength, is your goal, long sets should be an addition to your workout not the main focus.

2 - Medium Series (8 to 12 repetitions)

The theory of time under tension leads us to a third alternative: sets of 8 to 12 repetitions. At a pace of 2 seconds of concentric movement (the lift) and 2 seconds of eccentric movement (the descent), your set will end right in the optimal range of 30 to 60 seconds of tension time.

Why is this range important? Because, when the rep lasts longer than a few seconds, the body is forced to rely on the glycolytic system for energy, which leads to the formation of lactic acid. You might think that lactic acid is a bad thing, since it's mistakenly associated with the pain you can feel in the days after training. But, the pain produced by lactic acid is actually very fleeting and is vital for the production of new muscle tissue.

When lactic acid, or lactate, is produced in large amounts, it induces an increase in the levels of anabolic hormones throughout the body, which includes the all-important growth hormone and its sister, testosterone. These hormones, as they circulate, create a strong anabolic state. Now, if you are looking to gain muscle, this is exactly what you want.

3 - Short Series (5 repetitions or less)

In the world of bodybuilding a saying has passed the test of time: to be big, you have to be strong. Applying this to the extreme, many practitioners take a powerlifter approach, coupling very heavy loads to short sets. Look around in the weight room and you'll find an aspiring bodybuilder, or two, exhausting themselves on sets with near-maximum loads.

This method does build strength and, if you take a look at any talented powerlifter, you will notice that they have gained muscle mass with this workout. However, short sets have an important shortcoming: the stimulation of muscle fibers, and therefore growth, is closely related to the time the muscle spends under tension. Short sets of about 15 seconds or less will be the best to build strength, but they are also not as very effective at producing the growth of muscle sets of about 30 to 60 seconds long.

HOW TO MAXIMIZE HYPERTROPHY TO BUILD MUSCLE AS QUICK AS POSSIBLE

We practice weight training with the aim of gaining strength and to maximize hypertrophy to build muscle as quickly as possible. You know that you have to train hard, eat a diet rich in protein, low glycemic index carbohydrates and good fats, and that you must give your muscles time to rest in order to benefit from good muscle recovery. So, how do you maximize hypertrophy to build muscle as quickly as possible?

Volume
Volume is one of the main subjects when it comes to hypertrophy. It is the simplest factor you can use to build muscle mass. It simply means the amount of weight you lift throughout your whole workout. For example in one bench press set of 10 reps x 50kg you will lift a total volume of 500kg. Sounds like a lot right? Let's say you then bench press 60kg, which you will only probably lift about 6 times. That will give you a set volume of 360kg. Do you get my point?

Total workout volume is important because it is the easiest way to measure and track your progress, and the effect of your workout on muscle hypertrophy. The higher the volume, generally the higher the impact on hypertrophy. However, don't rule out shorter sets just yet as they help you improve your strength. More strength will lead you to putting more weight on the bar in your medium length sets, which again will increase your volume. We'll talk about that later.

Regeneration

This is the second of the two most important variables in hypertrophy. In order for your muscles to grow after a workout they NEED to regenerate. Your muscles don't actually grow during the workout(the pump you get during the workout is only temporary and completely wears of within 24 hours) but during regeneration time, which can be between 24 to 72 hours after the workout. The more advanced lifter usually regenerates quicker closer to the 24 hours. The more advanced you are the quicker you recover from a workout(and the shorter the soreness). Let's talk about the keys to good regeneration.

Sleep

Get a good night's sleep during your regeneration time of 7-8 hours of good quality sleep. 6 hours of good quality sleep is better than 9 hours of interrupted sleep. Your muscles regenerate the most during your sleep, therefore it is crucial to always sleep well following your workout.

Rich Diet

Increase your protein intake, with good quality protein(chicken breast, fish, nuts, beans etc.) and eat a very diversified healthy diet that will support your body and muscle growth with essential vitamins, nutrients, fatty acids, amino acids(the 20 building blocks of protein) and so on. The more nutrient dense your diet is, the better effect it will have on your muscle and strength.

Remember to eat good quality, diversified proteins like free range/ grass fed meat, fish, nuts or one of my secret favorite - hemp seeds (extremely nutritious!). Don't forget a sustainable source of carbohydrates like oats, quinoa, rice, bananas, potatoes(especially sweet potatoes), after your workout. Your muscles crave protein for regeneration and glucose from carbohydrates that you burnt during the workout. Having the two together is a great after work-out meal.

Do not overlook the good fats, especially the omega 3s, which improve insulin sensitivity in addition to reducing inflammation induced by training and protein consumption. Healthy sources of fat include: fish, eggs, nuts and seeds, olive oil, avocado(which I believe is a superfuit, contains all essential vitamins, minerals, protein, fats and fiber) etc.

Surprise The Muscles With Varying Stimulation

To promote muscle development in the context of bodybuilding, it is essential to impose two types of working routines: volume/ hypertrophy work and strength work. These two phases can be included in a long-term planning, where one plans, over several months (often two), the positioning of the heavy work and volume work: 1 heavy week and then 1 volume work week. You can also choose to use the two types of work together in one workout.

THE DIFFERENT METHODS TO MAXIMIZE BUILDING MUSCLES

High Eccentric Load Method

We will talk about the eccentric phase a bit more later. For now just remember that this is the part of the movement where you usually drop the weight down. The key is to control the weight down and not drop it. In the high eccentric load method you extend that eccentric phase to 3 to 5 seconds. This training strategy is based on the fact that eccentric contraction has the ability to generate greater muscle force during maximum contraction (approximately + 20-60%) compared to other types of contraction. Remember to use it in some of your sets during your workouts. The use of the eccentric phase of movement has been associated with exercise-induced microscopic "muscle tearing" and high strain, which has been associated with a high hypertrophic response. This stress from muscle tearing forces the body to regenerate muscles and build them stronger than they were before. This method also lets you learn appropriate technique during lifting as you will go slower and have the chance to focus on your form.

Cluster Sets / Super Sets

Another technique which partly balances both mechanical tension and metabolic stress consists of grouped series or "cluster sets". This consists of performing 2 or 3 sets with a limited rest time of only 10 to 20 seconds between each set to really pump up the muscles.

Try to finish off your workout with one or two series of super sets and see and feel the crazy pump you get in your arms! Super sets are best performed on smaller muscle parts and additional exercises like bicep dumbbell curls rather than complex exercises like the bench press.

CHAPTER 2: STRENGTH EQUALS HYPERTROPHY AND HYPERTROPHY EQUALS STRENGTH?

Many people start a strength training program without knowing exactly what the program should do for them over the long term. For a beginner, most well-constructed workout routines will get them results. This is because the body is not yet used to resistance training and will begin to adapt no matter what type of exercise is performed. On the other hand, the more an athlete (whether amateur or with the aim of becoming professional) becomes advanced in his training, the more training must be adapted to his objectives in order to achieve the desired results. Indeed, many beginners see a lot of results in the first months of training and then see their results stagnate without really understanding the causes of their plateau. This cause is often a program ill-suited to their goals. To understand which type of program to choose, it is important to understand the difference between the concepts of hypertrophy and muscular strength.

STRENGTH

In training, the term "strength" can be summarized as the maximum load that a person can lift. Strength training therefore focuses on being able to lift as much weight as possible without necessarily taking into account time constraints or the number of repetitions. This type of training therefore often includes exercises using a barbell and the basic movements requiring the participation of several muscles, ligaments and joints at the same time (eg: bench press, squat, deadlift, shoulder press), as opposed to.

There are often fewer repetitions of each exercise and fewer sets to perform. If you want to build strength you should focus on 2 to 4 sets of 1 to 6 maximum repetitions per exercise, with 1 to 2 exercises per muscle group. Of course, some programs will deviate slightly from this framework but most strength training programs will use this method to achieve maximum results.

The goal of this type of program is strictly to get stronger and increase the 1RM(1 Rep Maximum) weight. Strength and hypertrophy go hand in hand, not only can you build muscle and gain strength simultaneously, these two things are complementary. With bigger muscles comes the opportunity to gain strength and with more strength comes the ability to build more muscle. The key thing to distinguish here is that muscle size is not always equal to strength, hypertrophy training will increase muscle size but not so much strength. Strength training will increase muscle strength but not so much muscle mass. You can choose to focus on one or the other more effectively or try to develop both equally.

Strength Training

This type of training to gain strength has specific characteristics:
- The duration of the exercises is not essential.
- The important thing is the intensity of execution.
- We choose very heavy weights.
- We are working at 80% maximum weight load, that is to say close to failure.
- This is why there will be few repetitions.
- The rest between sets is long to regain strength (90+ seconds).

- We usually perform 3 sets of each exercise with a maximum of 5 repetitions. However sets of 3 repetitions can be extremely effective as well.

Hypertrophy/volume training

- It is necessary to manage to stress the muscle so that it increases its mass.
- More repetitions in most sets 6-15, to increase volume.
- There are more sets, to increase volume even more
- The weights are lower, to be able to lengthen the time of the exercise.
- The rest between sets is short, to keep the muscle under stress and blood flowing to it.
- Remember to make use of high eccentric load and cluster sets.
- Starting your hypertrophy workout with 1 or 2 lower rep strength sets(after warming up on lower weights) can be very beneficial to activate close to 100% muscle fibers for your further volume sets, or more.

Progressive Overload - The Key To Progress In Strength

Progressive overload is a system used to build both strength and muscle mass that will take your progress to the next level. To use this system you will need to write down all your performance(the exercise, weight and amount of reps and sets) either in a notepad or on your phone during your workouts. Ideally every session you want to add weight to your lifts and try to perform the same amount of reps and sets you did last week.

The key is to add as little weight as possible(2.5kg or less) to the bar, or whatever equipment you're using, so that you don't stagnate during the first week. This system is priceless when it comes to making progress in your training, and you will find all professionals and many dudes (and girls) in the gym using it. This will give you a plan that ensures you make progress over your training course.

If you struggle to lift the additional weight on the bar, choose to add either reps or sets to your exercises rather than weight. The main point here is to force progress, to "overload" your muscles, to which they will have to adapt and grow stronger and bigger. As long as your workout is "more" than it was last week, you've made progress.

Recapitulative Note:
By the end of this chapter, we should know that one of the most important basics of hypertrophy vs strength is to set your goals, whether you want to get bigger or stronger. Furthermore, know that one needs a bit of the other - a little bit of muscle mass training will help build strength, and the other way around a bit of strength training will help hypertrophy training as gaining strength will help you put more weight on the bar and increase your volume e.g. lifting 50kg x 10 vs 60kg x 10. The latter gives more volume.

CHAPTER 3:
TECHNIQUE IS KEY

The most common mistake to beginners in bodybuilding is to neglect the technique (also called form) of performing the exercises. Without learning the basics of bodybuilding (good technique for performing movements, defining a coherent training plan, respecting rest times, healthy eating) it is impossible to cross the substantial steps in bodybuilding leading to muscle gains having the effect of transforming our bodies.

However, the main reason hindering the progress of beginners when it comes to weightlifting is the failure to respect the technique of performing bodybuilding movements. Not respecting the technique of performing the movements has several bad consequences.

With regards to the quality of working out; you should always focus on "quality over quantity". How you lift weights might mean the distinction between making progress or just wasting your time. Beginners and newbies need to give time to learning legitimate structure before they can go on to lifting heavier weights and performing more advanced movements. Learning the appropriate form first is crucial to accelerating your performance.

Indeed, even the more experienced and advanced lifters profit from some intermittent structure criticism.

Appropriate Form Decreases The Probability Of Injury

Helpless structure places excessive loads on the ligaments, joints and tendons prompting strains and injuries. Great forms and mechanics decrease overcompensation and the probability of injury. You should focus on working and holding the weight with your muscles not resting it on your joints. Remember not to straighten your joints completely at the end of a movement, so you don't stress your joints e.g. straightening your arms completely at the top of the bench press movement.

Better Effectiveness

Why work more earnestly when you can work more brilliantly? Legitimate structure assists you with working out more proficiently so you can utilize your energy for the additional push rather than squandered developments.

Sharpen Your Concentration

Ill-advised forms and structure might mean you are focusing on accidental muscles. The better your structure and form is, the better your outcomes.

Remain Safe To Avoid Regressing

Remember to always make your lifting form your priority when training. Not only will this accelerate your progress but also protect you from stagnation. Inappropriate form can lead to injuries, which in term can lead to you losing your progress and having to stop training until you recover.

Instructions To Learn Appropriate Form:

In a perfect world, you will work with a personal trainer to begin with, who will teach you these appropriate techniques. Just be sure to choose someone who is actually trained in coaching people. Your trainer can screen your developments and reposition your body depending on the situation until the right structure turns out to be natural.

If you can't have a personal trainer, always try to use a mirror and your phone camera when lifting, to notice your structure. You will be surprised how different your form might look from a third person perspective and how much you can improve by having and utilizing that viewpoint.

BASIC WEIGHT TRAINING SAFETY TECHNIQUES

Training in a weight room in the gym requires some precautions. Also, certain rules must be observed to protect your body from injuries and overtraining. And here are some of the most important safety techniques:

- **Valsalva Maneuver**

The Valsalva maneuver involves forcefully inhaling into the stomach and then tightening your core before the lift. This technique traps air in your lungs and creates pressure inside your abdomen, called "intra-abdominal pressure," which stabilizes your torso against heavy loads. Typically, weightlifters use the Valsalva maneuver to prevent their spine from bending during exercises like the squat, deadlift, and bench press. It's important to utilise it in all weights exercises to keep your spine safe.

Why do weightlifters use the Valsalva maneuver?

Practitioners use the Valsalva maneuver because it helps them lift more weight. As the lungs expand, they put pressure on your back, internal organs, and chest, which helps your torso resist flexing or shifting when you are carrying heavy weights. Imagine that your upper body is a large cylinder, like a can of soda. When the box is empty (you don't have a lot of air in your lungs) it's relatively easy to bend down. When the can is full (there is air in the lungs), it is difficult to crush the can.

- **Preventing Weight Training Injuries**

Unfortunately, not all injuries are predictable. Accidents happen and you may be injured even if you take all precautions. Nevertheless, here are some tips to limit the risks:

- **Always Warm Your Whole Body And Especially The Shoulders Before Working The Upper Muscles.**

Start every workout with a quick warm up involving a short cardio and a stretch. You can also add in mobility and muscle activation work. A good warm up increases your performance significantly and reduces chances of injury.

- **Consider Strengthening The Back Of The Shoulders**
The rear deltoid is a muscle too often neglected which will however prevent you from a lot of pain. It will give you stability in exercises like the bench press. We'll cover how to strengthen it later.
- **Pay Attention To Your Back**
Protect your back by strengthening your abs and lower back, and always be sure to protect the lower back when handling loads. The back is the most complex muscle chain and also the most fragile if we do not take adequate measures to protect it. An injury quickly happens and those with chronic back pain know how essential it is to protect your back when practicing sports. So, follow these few tips to avoid back pain:

- ✓ Always keep your back straight and do not round your lower back when carrying heavy loads or when bending down to pick up a dumbbell or barbell.
- ✓ During leg workouts, warm up your ankles well to improve flexibility and avoid transmitting the entire load to the lower back.
- ✓ Work your abs and your lower back in the same session. These muscles are antagonistic and protect the lower back.
- ✓ Feel free to wear a weight belt for heavy core exercises such as squats, deadlights, and even bench presses.

- **Retracting Shoulders**

Retracting your shoulders is the main safety technique you will need to remember to use when doing most of your upper body exercises. This technique ensures your shoulders are locked in place in a safe position, that will not wear the joints and cause injury. This is crucial to perform as shoulder injuries are one of the most common in weightlifting.

Before getting into position, pull your shoulders back behind you, and down towards your waist, while contracting your back muscles. Throughout the lift keep your shoulders locked tightly in this position.

In certain exercises, specifically back exercises like the barbell row or pullup, you can choose to retract your shoulders before a repetition and loosen them after the repetition and retract them again before another rep, and keep doing that with every rep you do. This does take some practice but is a great way to strengthen your back muscles responsible for retracting your shoulders - the middle trapezius (commonly called traps) and rhomboid muscles. This is very important to learn to build a strong and balanced back that will keep your shoulders safe. Just remember not to do that in exercises that require your shoulders to be retracted all the time like the bench press!

You should use this technique in almost all of your exercises to protect your back. One of the most important exercises you want to really focus on utilizing this technique are: the deadlift, bench press, barbell row, pullups, shoulder press and bicep curls and many more!

- **"Snapping The Bar"**

This technique is applied to help you protect your elbow joints and activate your tricep and chest muscles. Most commonly used in upper body exercises like the bench press or shoulder press, but can also be used in exercises like the deadlift.

After retracting your shoulders and gripping the barbell, put pressure on it by trying to twist your wrists and arms inwards like if you were to try to snap the bar. This technique will keep your elbows safe and close to your body rather than flaring away from it. You want to avoid having your elbows flaring away from your body as it will create a greater angle in the elbows and put more pressure on the joints. While doing this in "push" exercises like the bench press, focus on contracting your triceps and chest to take even more weight off of the joints.

The most important exercises to perform this technique in are: most push (chest, shoulders, triceps) exercises - the bench press, shoulder press, pushups, tricep extensions etc. Furthermore, you should perform this technique to some extent in pull (back, biceps) exercises like the barbell row and pullups, which will help you to protect your elbows and work your biceps more.

- **Knees And Feet Out**

Follow this procedure to activate your leg muscles during leg exercises and take pressure off your joints. During leg exercises push your knees outwards, not inwards where the weight of the bar will pull them in. This will take the pressure off your knees and activate your hamstrings and glutes more.

To further help your posture you will need to protect from the weight causing your feet to become flat. You want to stand firmly on them spreading the weight equally through your foot sole. To avoid flat feet and help bring your knees out "twist" your feet outwards. Imagine you are trying to tear the ground in between your legs apart. This will stop you from having flat feet during your lifts but also further help you keep your knees out. These techniques will also make the lifts more comfortable to you by putting your legs out of your way when you are squatting/deadlifting.

CHAPTER 4: THE RULES TO FOLLOW - GETTING STARTED

- **Rule n°1: Choose The Right Sports Outfit:**

Choose a comfortable workout outfit that you feel comfortable in and reserve a pair of athletic shoes that you will only wear in the weight room. Above all, choose an outfit where you feel comfortable. Shorts, t-shirt and sneakers are ideal. Also, leggings and bras are perfect for women. In any case, never train in jeans or a shirt, this will impair your mobility.

Training footwear is very important, especially in leg workouts. You want to choose shoes that have a strong sole, that doesn't get compacted under weight easily (avoid the Airmaxes!) and ideally is higher at the heel than the toes, as this will give you a better angle for activating your leg muscles.

- **Rule n° 2: Warm Up**

Warm up before weight training. Warming up is essential to building muscle, but also to avoid injury. You can't go straight into a good workout without first warming up your body and muscles. Know that training without warming up exposes you to serious injuries: muscle tears, strains, tendonitis, and heart problems for violent cardio efforts. Warm up for 15 minutes before every weight session.

- **Rule n°3: Stay Hydrated**

Hydrate to improve your performance. Drink before you feel thirsty! Hydrating optimizes muscle growth in addition to allowing the body to eliminate toxins produced during exercise. 1% dehydration is 1% less performance. Don't wait until you're thirsty to drink, and get in the habit of drinking small sips in between sets. However, do not over hydrate yourself to the point it's making it difficult for you to lift.

- **Rule n°6: Be Careful With Weight Training Equipment**

Do not start a series before having first without having adjusted your bench/machine you are using. Then adjust the load you are going to handle. Always start with a light load and do a long set (20 reps), then gradually increase the load.

- **Rule n°6: Don't Overdo It**

Do not force too much in weight training. 1h15 is the average duration of an effective and efficient bodybuilding session. Beyond that, you expose yourself to overtraining and injury. Each consequent set you perform on a muscle group has a smaller impact on muscle hypertrophy and a higher chance of causing you injury. Stick to the recommended amount of sets per session that we will cover in the chapter on planning.

Never start a series until failure at the start of the session. After warming up, gradually increase the loads and difficulties. Go to muscle failure on one exercise and then move on to another. 3-5 weekly sessions of 75 minutes is a good average. There's no need to go beyond that. Furthermore, don't even add more than 5kg onto the bar if you have never tried that weight before, be patient and focus on form and remember it's your priority!

- **Rule n° 7: Spare Your Joints**

Pay attention to your joints. An injury is the best way to slow your muscle growth. Save your joints to optimize your progress in weight training. Wearing protective reinforcements on the wrists, elbows, knees or even the weight belt are not enough to protect your joints. To protect your joints:

✓ Warm up properly

✓ If you have a problem with an exercise or cause discomfort, leave it aside and choose another one. Many practitioners are injured because they think certain exercises are essential (bench press, row bar, straight bar curl, deadlift, etc.). All exercises have at least one equivalent. If an exercise puts too much pressure on a joint, it's not for you at the moment, seek advice on how to correct your form.

✓ Focus on "working the muscles" and keeping the weight off of the joints.

- **Rule n° 8: Keep Your Body Balanced**

Work all muscle groups. Don't overlook any muscle group. This harms the aesthetics of the body on the one hand, but be aware that a lagging muscle group = stagnation of all other muscle groups!

The body is an extremely balanced machine. If you build up one muscle group and leave others behind, you risk unbalancing your physique, and also injuring yourself. Also, the fact of not training one muscle group like the others can just hold you back from making any progress. Also remember one of the old school bodybuilding rules: <u>the muscles at the back of your body are the "backbone" of your physique</u>. Having strong back muscles, triceps, glutes and hamstrings will protect you from injury.

- **Rule n° 9: Stretch Before As Well As After Every Workout**

To progress and optimize your muscle building, stretch after each session. Stretching after a workout speeds up the muscle recovery process, but it also helps to better eliminate the toxins produced during the session. Stretching is the best prevention against injury. Be careful, however, not to go to pain. Stretch gently. When lifting weight your muscles will often stiffen up so it's important to stretch after the sessions to keep your body flexible. A flexible body is less prone to injuries.

- **Rule n° 10: Find The Right Supplements For Best Results**

One good example are BCAAs (Branched-chain amino acids): amino acids that our bodies aren't able to build from other amino acids in the diet. It can be beneficial to supplement these, because if you don;t get enough in your diet, this could slow down your protein synthesis. Food supplements help provide muscles with all the nutrients they need for optimal muscle building.

A balanced diet rich in proteins, complex carbohydrates and essential fatty acids is one of the conditions for obtaining good muscle growth but also for muscle definition. Food supplements are specifically designed to fill all the nutrient and macronutrient deficiencies that athletes may encounter. Here are the food supplements that we will help you:

✔ **Powdered proteins**: whey, casein, and vegetable proteins are practical and faster digestible than the proteins found in "solid" food. Adding a protein shake to your daily food intake provides you with the protein quota necessary for muscle growth.

✔ **Creatine:** One of the most tested fitness supplements and therefore considered one of the safest. Creatine creates a enviroment in the muscles that is beneficial for hypertrophy and increased training performance (don't worry it is not a steroid)

✔ **Vitamins and minerals:** it is essential to provide the body with the right amount of vitamin C, group B vitamins, as well essential fatty acids and minerals and antioxidants necessary for basic recovery. These can have a great effect on your muscle hypertrophy.

TYPES OF MUSCLE CONTRACTIONS: CONCENTRIC, ECCENTRIC AND ISOMETRIC

There are various types of contractions that you should know if you want to start weightlifting and that are the most common among bodybuilders. To put it simply, when working the biceps, the moment you curl is the <u>concentric phase</u> and the moment you pull the weight down is the <u>eccentric phase</u>. It's important to be aware of these contractions as you can use them to your advantage when lifting weights, to achieve better results. And here are the most important types of muscle contractions:

CONCENTRIC CONTRACTION

During the concentric phase, the two ends of the muscle come closer to each other and the muscle gains in size. Also called the positive phase, this contraction is the most commonly focused on and thought to be the most important but the eccentric phase is actually as important, if not more. The faster you perform the concentric phase, the more difficult it is, therefore the better the results. The concentric phase should be performed at a decent tempo, however not too fast to avoid injury.

THE ECCENTRIC
CONTRACTION

During the eccentric phase, or negative phase, the two ends of the muscle move apart. If, without weight, this movement is completely natural and easy to perform, it is much less so when it is associated with a load. To take the example of the biceps curl, when we enter the negative phase (the moment when we go back down) while retaining the load, the muscle will contract while stretching.

During the eccentric phase, there will be a strong tension which will solicit muscle fibers different from those solicited during the concentric phase. This is why the two are complementary, even inseparable. Extending the eccentric phase puts good stress on the muscle and causes muscle fibers to "tear" which overtime strengthens and grows the muscle.

This contraction can be more effective in hypertrophy than concentric contractions. It is important to keep the muscle under constant tension in both the concentric and eccentric phase. Extending the eccentric phase is an extremely effective method used to avoid stagnation in hypertrophy. You should aim to make your eccentric phase last at least 3 seconds or more in most of your exercises. You can also finish your workouts with even longer eccentric phases of 5-10 seconds. Pulling the weight down slowly is a great way to further strengthen your muscles.

ISOMETRIC CONTRACTION

Unlike other contractions, this one does not require any joint movement, and therefore does not cause any change in the length of the muscle (stretching, contraction). The goal is therefore to achieve a powerful and voluntary contraction, without making the slightest movement. The best example of this way of working is sheathing/the plank. During this contraction the muscle stays contracted all the time, therefore this contraction hasn't got such great benefits for hypertrophy.

However utilizing this contraction can still be very useful as it trains endurance of the muscle, which can be very important in training the core muscles for example. This is very important as good core strength is necessary to perform compound exercises like the deadlift, squat or barbell row. Practicing the plank is a great way to strengthen the core to avoid injury in compound exercises.

PLYOMETRIC CONTRACTION

Plyometric contraction is the term used to name the combination of eccentric contraction immediately followed by dynamic concentric contraction. It is a working method which is primarily intended for athletes who wish to increase their power, however is also great for building muscle in general.

Note:

Each muscle contraction therefore makes it possible to work the muscle in a different way and thus to adapt your session according to your objectives:

- Muscle mass gain

- Increased strength

- Explosive development

- Improved muscular endurance

We can say that each type of contraction impacts muscle fibers in different ways. It is essential to take them into account when planning training. In conclusion, in the search for performance and progression of athletes it is important to adapt these tools to the needs of each one while increasing the loads in progressive overload and thoughtful ways for the achievement of their objective.

CHAPTER 5: WEIGHTLIFTING STEPS:

Start With a Quick Warm Up

Warming up is a must before a weights session. First of all, remember that the primary interest of warming up is to prepare your body for the effort and therefore to limit the risk of injury, a second advantage of warming up is that if it is done well, it can improve performance, raising the amount of reps and the weight you can lift. We talk about warming up because the goal is literally to raise the temperature of the muscles and the body, and to put them in an optimal state for the practice of a physical activity.

In addition, when the human body begins a physical effort, even of low intensity, the synovial fluid (or synovia) is secreted by the synovial membranes of the joints of (knee, elbow, ankle, hip, shoulder, etc.). Basically, your joints fill with a lubricating liquid which allows them to function better and reduce the frictional forces and the pressure undergone during exercise.

The intensity should be gradual during your warm up so you don't deplete your muscles from glucose they will need during the lifts. Here are the steps to follow for your warm-up with a weight lifting session:

1. Systematically, start your workout with a cardiovascular warm-

up lasting 5 to 10 minutes on a bike, rower, treadmill or elliptical trainer.

2. Then, using a simple movement without load, mobilize each of your joints starting from the neck and going down all along the body (about ten movements per joint). For example, gently turn your head from side to side; do arm swings etc. The objective is to allow each joint to move as best as possible according to its anatomical possibilities. Carry on with some short stretches as well to loosen up your muscles and ligaments.

3. Begin the specific phase of the warm-up. It will depend mainly on your session and the muscle groups you will be working. If you want to optimize your performance during your training, you can include plyometric or ballistic movements (jumps, explosive pushes / pulls with elastic bands, etc.). The goal is to achieve movements that are closest to the exercise that will follow but with a stretch and contraction of the muscle at high speed. In a simple way, it prepares your nervous system for the effort.

4. Finally, you can start with your first exercise in the session, <u>always starting an empty bar</u> if using the barbell, and then gradually increasing the load until your workload. Aim for 10-15 reps in your warm up sets and focus on the movement, form and muscles involved.

WEIGHTLIFTING WARMING EXERCISES

1. Star Jumps

Star jumps are really perfect cardio exercises to warm the entire body in no time. You will quickly understand that star jumps have the ability to activate your legs, your abdominal strap, your chest and your heart rate at the same time.

2. High Jumps

This is a very simple exercise. You start standing with your feet together and your arms at your sides. Then jump up as high as you can, spread your legs wide and raise your arms in rhythm and at the same time. Return to your starting position and repeat. Keep your torso straight. For this exercise, you work the legs, arms, core, and cardio. You can do this at different paces and perform this exercise for a great warm-up.

3. Arm Swings

Arm swings are essential for all upper body sessions. Remember to perform all the variations: backwards, forwards, lateral, horizontal and you can even do alternating swings if you want.

4. Shoulder Rotations

As these are fairly fragile joints, these are parts of the body that must be warmed up before each session. Do shoulder rotations even if that is not the muscle group you are going to be working. During a weight training session, you will still use the shoulders, even for just moving the weights. It is a very simple movement which consists of spreading the arms and doing rotations in one direction, then in the other.

5. Bodyweight squats

Squat down bending in your hips first and as you squat down, then bend in the knees. Keep your back straight. Go down until your tights are parallel with the ground. Perform squats to warm the legs and core. Squats are a great way to warm up all of your whole body, especially the leg muscles. Bodyweight squats will also build your leg muscles quite well.

6. Push ups

The simplest and best exercise you can perform anywhere and at any time, which is what makes it so good, however probably undervalued by many.
Push ups are great to warm you up before bench pressing but are also great to progress and grow your chest and triceps long term. Remember to keep your shoulder tucked back and elbows slightly in to activate the triceps and the chest. Keep it steady on the way down, putting tension on these muscles. Furthermore, you can focus the triceps more by bringing your hands a bit lower and closer to your chest.

7. Skipping

A great warming exercise that can be a lot of fun as well. Don't be intimidated if you have never tried skipping the rope before you will pick it up fairly quickly. Overtime you can learn to do alternate, one-leg and double jumps to add a bit more fun to it. This great cardio exercise can help you work your calves as well, which most of us don't like doing in the gym.

8. Cardio Machines

All cardio machines like the treadmill, rower, elliptical cross trainer etc. are great to use for your warmup. Personally I like the rower the most as it is great for warming up the whole body including the shoulders and leg muscles. Use these to bring your body temperature up before your workout.

THE SIX CORE
MOVEMENTS

The core movements, called the primary or more commonly: compound movements. These should be the base of all strength training routines. The reason they are so good is because they target more than one muscle at a time in one exercise, saving you time during your workout. Furthermore, they are practical, natural moves that will make your whole body stronger and give you practical strength in real life situations.

All of the compound movements will strengthen your core. Just remember to go steady with these and increase the weight gradually as these are more technical movements and always focus on form/technique over the weight you put on the bar. Always remember to control the weight on the way down(eccentric phase), which will protect you from injuries, keep good form and work your muscles more.

- **DEADLIFT**

The king of the core movements, works all your body muscles but mainly the leg and back muscles.
Remember to perform the valsalva maneuver before every rep, to protect your back and keep your core as tight as you can to protect your back. Before lifting, retract your shoulders and push your chest out. Make sure your bar travels straight up and straight down, not around your knees or to the back as you're pulling with your glutes.

As with most leg exercises push your knees outwards not inside, where the weight will usually pull your knees. This will protect your knee joints and activate the glutes and hamstrings to give you more power. Start by just pulling the bar upwards with the power of your legs and as the bar passes roughly the height of your knees, start pulling with your glutes. For some people this will be a bit higher or lower depending on the length of your limbs.

When you lift the bar, remember not to yank/jerk the weight upwards rapidly but rather start slow and increase your pull until you lift the bar off the floor. This is really important as pulling heavy weight vigorously can hurt your back. You can choose to either drop the weight down, letting it go off your hands or put it down slowly, in a controlled movement, to benefit from the eccentric phase.

During this exercise your back should be perfectly straight, not arched either backwards or forwards. Pay special attention to your lower back. Activate all of your back muscles to strengthen your posture. Make sure you are standing firmly on your feet and spreading the weight out evenly on them. You can use a lifting belt in this exercise to protect your back if you want.

Try different variations like the sumo deadlift or the Romanian deadlift. In the Romanian variation you keep your legs almost straight all the time after you lift the bar off the floor with just a little bend in your knees. Keep your back straight and lower your chest down until the bar reaches your knees level and then pull back up. Keep the weight lower as these variations are more challenging. This variation also targets the hamstrings really heavy compared to a standard deadlift.

- **SQUAT**

Main muscles: quadriceps, glutes and hamstrings.

Use the same principles as described in the deadlift, valsalva maneuver, tight core and knees out. To begin with, use a squat rack and place the bar on your back, on top of your trapezius(traps) muscles to perform the standard high-bar squat.

A low-bar squat is where you put the bar under the bones of your shoulders. This variation will have you lean over more and target the glutes and hamstrings more. Most people will be able to squat a bit more weight using this variation but start learning with the high-bar squat first.

To squat, first perform the valsalva maneuver, then bend in your hips first taking the weight in your hips and leg muscles, including the hamstring and glutes. Then, as you begin to squat down with the bar, bend in your knees, keeping them outwards. Remember to make sure the bar travels straight down and straight up. You only need to squat down to a 90 degree angle between your legs and calves or laps parallel with the ground. On the way down focus on controlling your weight with the hamstrings and glutes, and really activating these muscles to keep the pressure off your lower back.

Same as with the deadlift: keep your back straight and back and core muscles very tight. Stand firmly on your feet and use a lifting belt if you want to.

You can also try the front squat variation to target the quads more. Rather than retracting your shoulders pull them out in front off you and place the bar on them underneath your chin. Keep the weight low as this is a challenging exercise, start with just the bar with no plates and train until you feel comfortable. This variation is a lot more demanding of the core strength.

- **PULL-UPS**

Main muscles: latissimus dorsi, commonly called lats, which are the wider back muscles.

Secondary muscles: biceps muscles

This is one of your two main exercises for the back muscles and the biceps. There are 4 main variations a standard overhand grip pull-up being your main one, underhand pull-ups (done no wider than shoulder width for safety), chin-ups, that target the biceps more, and hammer grip pull-ups done using two parallel bars that target the back muscles the most out of all the variations.

If you're not strong enough yet to do pull-ups, start with either lat pulldown machines or do just the eccentric phase of the pull-up using a gym box to grab onto the bar and lower yourself slowly. Using this method you will progress fast and be able to do a full pull-up within a few sessions.

During the pull-ups you should keep your shoulders retracted all the time to begin with. However, you do want to learn to release them as you pull yourself down and then retract them before you pull up again. This is really important to completely train your back muscles and the strength of your shoulder blade retracting muscles. Also remember to pull yourself down controllably, extending your eccentric and sparing your joints and ligaments from dropping all your weight down on them.

- **BENCH PRESS**

Main muscles: pectoral muscles - chest muscles

Secondary muscles - triceps and front deltoid

Using a bench, bar and a bar rack you can perform the most important chest exercise, the bench press. Your contact points are your feet, glutes and shoulders. First place your feet firmly on the ground close to the bench, tuck your shoulders back and place them tight on the bench forming a slight arch in your back between your glutes and shoulder. Forming this arch is very important to keep your shoulders safe.

Second, tighten up and perform the valsalva maneuver, remember to keep the core and the back muscles tight. Lift the bar off the rack and hold it right over your shoulders and press it down to your lower chest (on a slight incline, not straight down). Then push the bar back up the same trajectory returning it over the shoulders. Remember to keep your elbows tucked in towards your body not flaring away from you to activate your chest and triceps. With your hands try to "snap" the bar, which will again naturally keep your elbows tucked in and keep the chest and triceps muscles more activated.

- **ROWING**

Main muscles: All back muscles, mainly lats.
Secondary muscles: the biceps and rear deltoids
Remember to keep your elbows tucked in during this exercise. Pick the back up either off the ground by performing a deadlift or off the lowest point on the bar rack to make your life easier. Keeping your arms straight down, lean down to between 45 to 75 degree angle in your hips.

A lesser lean will target your lat muscles and a stronger lean will target your upper back muscles more including the rear deltoids. When in position, pull the bar towards your back with your arms, as if you were rowing, up to your stomach. Focus on using your back muscles and the biceps to pull the bar towards your back and don't swing your whole body, work just the muscles. You can also try one-handed rowing with a dumbbell leaning on a inclined bench.

- **SHOULDER PRESS/MILITARY PRESS**

Main muscles: deltoids - shoulder muscles.
Secondary muscles - triceps
What we call "military press" is your main shoulders exercise. This is quite an advanced exercise that many can find quite challenging

to perform properly without pain. Therefore, go light, just a 20kg bar is enough to start with and see significant progress with.

In the beginning of the shoulder press the bar arrives in front of your face, at a level where you have a 90 degree angle in your elbows not down to your collarbones(to spare your joints). The bar is pressed straight upwards, while pulling your head back away from the bar, not drawing the bar around your head (a very common mistake). Apply your tricep strength when pressing the bacr upwards and when slowly pulling the weight down.

Be sure to warm up your shoulders properly before this exercise and go easy on the weight as this is quite a demanding movement. Remember you should keep your back perfectly straight and the core very tight throughout the move.

Note:

For all of these exercises it is best to perform them without a bar or any weight first for a warmup and then increase the weight every set, best by no more than 5 kg (2 x 2.5kg plates) a set to start with. Remember to keep your core very tight in all compound movements to protect the lower back.

MORE ADVANCED MOVES

The snatch and the clean and press are typical weightlifting moves you may see in the olympics. They are more advanced and should be attended only after you have gained confidence in the 6 core movements. Both of the moves give great benefits in increased mobility, core stability and overall body strength. The main muscles worked are the leg muscles, core, back and shoulders.

Snatch
Start in a deadlift position with your hands placed with a wide grip on the bar, possibly on the ends of it, if you can reach. Keeping your arms straight pull the bar off the ground vigorously and upwards. You're going to perform a snatch and lift the bar over your head into an overhead press position. While holding the weight over your head, go into a deep squat. Once you gain stability, squat up. To finish the move you can just drop the weight in front of you while stepping out of the way of the bar.

The more dynamically you perform the move the easier it is going to be for you, it is all about the flow and form. Obviously remember perform the valsalva maneuver and keep your core very tight before the lift and keep your back straight

Clean and Press
Similar to the snatch but more advanced. You should start the lift

in a deadlift position with a natural grip of shoulder's width. For beginners, you may choose to start in a squat and place the bar on your tights or on the hips.

As with the snatch, lift the bar up off the ground vigorously but going into a standing front squat position(place the bar on your collar bones and front shoulders). Don't go into a full squat but rather stay upwards with a little bend in your knees. When you're ready push the bar up performing an overhead press, pushing up with your legs for additional drive power. Some lifters will step one of their legs behind them going into a lunge position, which helps them to push the bar over their head. Again, keep your core tight and protect your back.

Note:
Perform these exercises with just an empty bar to begin with and practice until you feel comfortable with it and add no more than 5kg at a time. These two moves can be very rewarding but also harmful if not done correctly. Finally, as always, remember about core stability and use a lifting belt if you want to.

ADDITIONAL EXERCISES

Secondary exercises are used to add volume to your training, hit your muscles from a different angle and target muscles that the compound exercises don't focus on like the biceps or medial deltoids (side shoulders).

Incline Bench Press And Dumbbell Bench Press
Use an incline bench to target your top pectoral muscles. This exercise is very important to include in your every chest workout as without it you won't get a good looking well defined chest and the classic V-shape body structure because flat bench presses don't target the top pectorals very well.

Don't forget to try dumbbell presses as well to add variation to your workout, both on a flat bench and an incline. Dumbbells give you a bigger range of motion that the bar limits you from. Working in a larger range of motion can be beneficial to work your muscles more.

Chest Flies
Done either with dumbbells or on a cable machine. Start with arms straight above the chest. Simply slowly stretch your chest muscle by drawing your arms towards your back remembering to keep your elbows and shoulders tucked in. Then pull back with just the strength of your chest muscles.

Keep your arms curled just a little bit all the time but don't curl them any more during the lift, to avoid using your biceps strength during the concentric phase. Use just the chest strength and go very low with the weight and perform between 8 to 15 reps. This exercise is great to both warm up and end your chest workout.

Lat Pulldown / V-bar Pulldown

Lat pulldown machines are great to add volume to your back workouts. The movement is the same as with a standard pull up. Remember to keep your elbows tucked in and pull mainly with your back muscles(lats) not your arms. As with the standard pull up aim to learn to work your shoulder retracting muscles but you can start by keeping your shoulders retracted all the time at first. You can use different attachments to target the muscles differently like the V-bar to target the biceps more.

Lateral Raises

Essential to grow wider shoulders. Remember to keep your shoulders tucked in and down, keep the weight very low and work with just the lateral delt muscles, no swinging and cheating, keep the rep range high at 8-15 reps. Lean over a bit with dumbbells in your hand keeping them on the sides of your body. Raise your arms up sideways to the 90 degree level, forming a T with your body. Then slowly control the weight down focusing on the eccentric.

Bench Dumbbell Shoulder Press

Adjust your bench to a slight incline. Once again keep the shoulders tucked in. Your arms are meant to be flared at a 45 degree angle away from your body not fully out to protect your joints. Remember to try to tuck your elbows in to drive the weight through them. Start by lifting the arms up to a 90 bend in your elbows and press up. Control the weight on the way down and repeat. Remember to use your tricep strength the same as in the military press.

Bonus: Arnold Shoulder Press

Another variation of this exercise named after Arnold Shwarzeneger in which you start by bringing your arms and dumbbells forwards in front of your face, your palms facing towards you. To start the movement bring your arms outwards to your sides and then perform the press. Go back down and then bring your arms back to the starting position in front of your face.

Lunges
Done either with just bodyweight or light dumbbells, place one leg forward and squat down on it then come up and do the same with the other leg and carry on along a long stretch in your gym. You can also do this standing in place with just one leg at a time. This exercise is great for targeting the glutes and quads. Again remember to push the knees out to flex the glutes and keep the core tight.

Bicep Curls
Done with either a barbell or dumbbells. Remember to use reasonable weights and work with just your biceps and forearms strength (don't swing with your whole body like you will see some people do in the gym). When curling you can push your elbows out in the direction you're facing a little bit, which is also a function of the bicep muscle. Just don't over do it.

Use different grip variations like the hammer curls and both dumbbells and barbells to hit your biceps from different angles. When doing standard dumbbell biceps curls twist your hand outwards towards the end of the move to further activate your biceps. You can try it now and feel your biceps tense with no weight.

The bicep is made of two heads: the long head and the short head. Remember to target both during your workouts. Hammer curls and close grip curls will target your long bicep head more, which is usually the one that is worked less by most.

Triceps
One of the best exercises for the triceps are close grip bench press and close grip pushups. They're great because they're technically a

compound movement and will still target multiple muscles, while focusing on the triceps.

Other than that the best additional exercises are triceps extensions which look like the opposite of a biceps curl. Use over and under-hand grip and different variations like the overhead tricep extension to target all three tricep heads. You can perform these extensions using a bar or cable machines.

To perform with a bar, raise it over your head first. Starting with the arms straight, bend in your elbows and lower the bar slowly behind your head to about 45 degree angle. Then push the bar back up and repeat. You can do the same using a cable machine or do tricep pushdowns in front of your body rather than overhead presses.

Rear Delts Raise
Done with either dumbbells or on a cable machine. The exercise looks like the opposite of the chest fly. Bend over with dumbbells in your hand and arms straight. Keeping your arms straight draw them up towards your back, forming a T with your body. Once again keep your Shoulders and elbows tucked in all the time. This exercise requires the lowest weight out of all the exercises covered and can be very difficult to perfect for a lot of people. There's no need to go heavier than 5-10kg.

Note:
Do not undervalue this last exercise. It is very important to strengthen your rear delts to keep your shoulders strong and safe during your lifts. Furthermore, defined read delts give you fuller shoulders and a cannon-like shoulders look!

CHAPTER 6:
WEIGHTLIFTING
AND DIET

We have touched upon the concept of a balanced diet before, which you need to follow to give your body the appropriate nutrients for your muscles to thrive. Now I would like to touch on the concept of calories and how much you should eat to achieve your goals

Calorie Needs And Balance

Just as a car needs gasoline to run, our body needs energy to live and perform everyday tasks. This energy is measured in calories, but since they are counted by the thousands, we use the term kilocalorie (= 1000 calories) which we denote by kcal or Cal (with a capital C). Our energy consumption can usually be divided into about two main needs for our body:

The basic metabolism: it is the minimum energy the body burns in a day to maintain vital functions, like a parked car whose engine is running;

There are other energy needs such as thermoregulation and digestion, but we have chosen not to complicate unnecessarily.

Basal metabolism varies enormously from one individual to another: it depends on age, sex, weight, thyroid activity, etc. It can be twice as big for a growing teenager as it is for an adult. The sum of basal metabolism and other energy requirements is Total Metabolism, which is the total energy you consume in a day.

Calorie Surplus / Bulk

This term is used to describe when somebody eats more calories than their body burns. If you want to achieve that you should eat 300-500 kcal over your basal metabolism. Beyond that, the extra calories are likely to form body fat, which helps to build muscle.

After training, stressed muscles go through repair and construction processes. This "muscle protein synthesis" lasts between 24 and 72 hours depending on the intensity of the training. This means that you need to rest the muscle group in the range of 24 to 72 hours before you train it again. But it also means that with 2 to 4 training sessions per week, muscle protein synthesis takes place almost continuously. This is why you must ensure, every day, to provide your body with enough protein and to achieve a sufficient caloric surplus.

To find out how many calories you should be consuming, to use an online calculator that will show you how many calories you should be eating a day. Simply type in Google: calorie calculator. Such a calculator should let you put in your: gender, age, height and weight as well as your physical activity to show you how much calories you should be consuming. To the amount given by the calculator either add or subtract 300-500 calories a day to achieve your goals of either losing or gaining weight.

In order to give only an average figure, the average total metabolism of an adult man (average height and weight) is about 2500 Kcal. Then playing sports in general, but more particularly in bodybuilding / bodybuilding and weight training, diet plays a vital role in achieving your goals.

Caloric deficit

In order to lose weight you will need to eat less calories than your calculated calorie expenditure. This is called a caloric deficit.

MAIN MACRONUTRIENTS NEEDED FOR HYPERTROPHY

The three macronutrients found in foods are:

➤ Proteins,

➤ Lipids,

➤ Carbohydrates

The normal ratio of macronutrients is around 30% protein, 40% carbohydrate, and 30% fat. This percentage is to be understood in terms of calorie intake and not in weight. Be careful to read the labels carefully. Let's give you a quick overview of these nutrients.

- Proteins

Proteins are certainly the most famous nutrient in bodybuilding, because they are involved in the (re) construction of the body. Protein is mainly found densely in products like meat, fish, eggs and dairy products. Legumes, nuts and seeds are great sources of protein rich in minerals and vitamins.

It is important to consume different forms of protein, both animal and plant sources, to supply your body with the whole spectrum of amino acids it needs. You will find the best quality proteins in whole foods, not supplements like whey protein. Therefore, it is important to eat a nutrient dense diet and only use supplements to add to it.

The recommended daily intake for muscle growth is 1 gram of protein per 1 kg of your bodyweight, so if you weigh 70kg you should consume about 70 grams of protein a day to build muscle. You should stop yourself from eating unnecessary amounts of protein as some fitness "experts" will advise you to. Our bodies aren't able to absorb big amounts of protein and it becomes toxic to our body as it has to get rid of the excess, straining the whole digestive and urinary system, mainly the liver and kidneys. 70 grams a day should be absolutely enough for most people.

- Carbohydrates

Carbohydrates have an important energy role. In terms of Glycemic Index (GI), we can classify carbohydrates in 2 categories:

1. **High GI Carbohydrates:** sugar, honey, most fruit, potato fries
1. **Low GI Carbohydrates:** beans, sweet potatoes, lentils, rice, berries like blueberries, green bananas

Low GI carbohydrates should be favored, as they don't spike your insulin as much(which creates inflammation in the body) and they release glucose slowly and gradually to the body, creating a constant, good source of energy for the body.
High GI carbohydrates are preferred during intense efforts because they quickly provide energy. However, remember not to over consume them.

- Lipids

Lipids are fats. They have a bad reputation but are essential for good health. Fat is made up of saturated or unsaturated fatty acids. Foods contain different types of fatty acids, each with its own strengths and weaknesses. Thus, depending on the type and amount of fatty acids consumed, the effects will be different on your health.

- **Saturated Fats:** animal fat, dairy products, coconut, butter etc.
- **Unsaturated Fats:** fatty fish, vegetable oils, nuts, seeds, avocado etc.
- **Trans fats:** biscuits, crisps, pastries, fast food, etc.

Whether you are athletic or not, it is above all necessary to favor good quality fats, mainly unsaturated fats like: fish, avocado, olive oil etc. Saturated fat is actually okay, contrary to what the world used to believe about saturated fats, as long as the source is a healthy one e.g. coconut. However, trans fats should be always avoided as they are highly inflammatory.

Vitamins, Minerals And Other Phytonutrients

You absolutely cannot forget about micronutrients for building muscle and optimal health in general. Micronutrients are nutrients like vitamins and minerals but also thousands of phytonutrients like: bioflavonoids, polyphenols, carotenoids and many more.

Micronutrients are most dense in: fruit, vegetables, legumes like beans, nuts, seeds etc. but the best source of them are green vegetables, especially green leafy veggies.

Micronutrients are essential for our bodies to build muscle as they support muscle regeneration, good sleep, energy levels and overall health. Some of the most important vitamins for your muscles you might want to consider are: Vitamins: A, E, C, D and B vitamins. Out of the minerals the most important for you will be: zinc, calcium, magnesium and potassium. Some really rich sources of these nutrients are foods like: broccoli, spinach, avocado, dark chocolate (72%+), hemp seeds, flax seeds, beans, salmon and so on.

How many meals should I eat each day?

Muscle development is best stimulated if the body is continuously supplied with adequate nutrients. It is therefore better to absorb your quota of proteins and your ratio of calories in several meals spread over the day.

In general, I recommend that you eat about 3 to 4 nutrient dense meals. If there is a time to take in order to absorb protein, it is immediately after your session.

SUPPLEMENTS

Supplements help you achieve your training goals by adding nutrients that you didn't get enough of from your diet. Remember that they are only what the name suggests: supplements. They are not meant to replace your diet but only add to it. A solid, healthy and balanced diet is a key to great physique and no supplements can fix it.

Creatine
Creatine is a protein naturally found in meat, however in small amounts. Creatine increases water retention in the muscles, creating a beneficial environment for muscles to grow. It also increases strength by increasing ATP recovery, meaning you should have more energy and a bit more strength during your workouts.

This supplement is named "the safest" supplement in the industry as it is the most tested and natural supplement on the market. When used in normal dosage, creatine has no side effects and can actually have health benefits for the brain and kidneys.

There are various kinds of creatine, I recommend using 3-5 grams of creatine monohydrate daily, which is the choice of most athletes. Some athletes choose to do a creatine loading phase when they begin to take creatine. This is done to achieve a 100% satiety effect of creatine in the muscles as it normally takes about 2-3 weeks to achieve that with the standard dose. Creatine loading consists of taking a higher dose of creatine multiple times a day to bring the body satiety up to 100% quicker e.g. 5 grams, 3 times a day for a week, and then a normal dose daily afterwards.

Protein Powders

Protein powders are ultra filtered proteins that are digested quickly and usually contain no fat or sugar. Its speed of assimilation makes it an ideal food supplement to provide the muscles with a maximum of amino acids when they need them most: when getting up in the morning and after training. You can supplement protein powder on days when you haven't reached your target protein intake of 1 gram of protein per kg of bodyweight. My personal favourite is hemp protein powder as it has the best amino acid profile and is rich in various minerals and omega-3 fatty acids.

BCAAs

The BCAA are a combination of essential amino acids for muscle growth: leucine, isoleucine and valine. Leucine, the most anabolic of the 3 amino acids, is crucial for protein synthesis and therefore for supporting muscle anabolism. BCAAs can be important to supplement as they are the only 3 amino acids out of 20 that can't be built by our bodies from other amino acids that we eat. That's why they're called essential.

BCAAs can be taken up to three times a day. They are best taken around workout times either before or after, or both. You shouldn't need more than 5 grams of BCAAs a day, therefore you could choose to take 2.5 grams before and after a workout to supplement your protein synthesis.

Pre-Workouts

Pre-workouts, or nitrogen monoxide precursors, are formulas containing large amounts of arginine, AAKG and citrulline - 3 amino acids known to increase the production of nitric oxide, a gas that expands the walls blood vessels and not only reinforce muscle congestion, but also improve the transport of nutrients to the muscles. They usually contain a decent amount of caffeine as well.

You can use these supplements before a workout to give you a "kick" to fuel your workout.

My favorite pre-workout, however, is coffee. It is a natural and cheap form of a pre-workout and has no side effects that many pre-workout supplements do have from the unnatural, chemical compounds in them. Coffee will have similar benefits to your sessions as a pre-workout supplement, without the side effects. Furthermore, coffee is considered a "superfood" because of its impressive amounts of polyphenols, which you won't get from pre-workout powders.

CHAPTER 7: THE IMPORTANCE OF A PLAN

We will finish off the book with a chapter on the most important part of your weightlifting journey: your weekly plan. Without a plan your workouts won't be organized, therefore it is important to have a plan you can follow that will accelerate your progress. You also need to follow a plan to make sure you don't skip any of the muscle parts and put your body out of balance.

I won't give you an exact plan to follow as everyone is different and needs a different plan to their needs. However I will give you simple guides that you can follow, so you can easily create a workout plan that works specifically for you. Let's start with a few notes to keep in mind.

- **Be Specific**

Set exact goals of e.g. how much muscle you want to put on or how much do you want to bench press, and set deadlines. That will help you track your progress and adjust accordingly to your plan. Remember: the key to setting goals in whatever you do is to set the bar high so you aim for good results.

- **Decide The Number Of Sessions Per Week**

Plan the number of sessions per week according to your body-building goal. Training every day is not effective. Muscles and the nervous system need recovery in order to progress. The harder your workout the more time you will need to recover. For best results I recommend training 3-5 times a week.

- **Set The Weak Points To Improve**

Focus on your weak points for improvement. Sometimes, 2 sessions per week on a lagging muscle group can be enough to boost its growth. It's very important to develop weaker parts as they will cripple the growth of other muscle groups if not taken care of.

- **Weight And Physical Performance Evaluation**

Before establishing a plan of action, it makes sense to weigh yourself and assess your physical performance. I advise you to weigh yourself in the morning on an empty stomach and note your weight in a training log. Regarding your physical performance, evaluate your 1 RM (maximum repetition) and your 10 RM on the 3 basic movements (squat, deadlift and bench press) and note your performance in the training log. Don't forget to write the date.
- **Establish An Action Plan**

Establish an action plan that answers these 4 questions:
- ✓ What is my bodybuilding goal?
- ✓ What is my due date?
- ✓ Do I have weak points to catch up?
- ✓ How many sessions will I do per week?

After answering these 4 questions, plan an adapted sports and diet program. These will evolve according to your motivations and your performance. Above all, do not ignore the diet, which in my opinion corresponds to 50% of the results.

Even if your due date is set, go step by step by tracking your progress each week. For example, if you want to lose 12 kg in 6 months, focus on losing a kilo every 2 weeks. I advise you to open a training log by writing down your weight and your performance every week. You should also use your phone to take pictures of the progress.

- **Amount Of Sets In a Week Per Muscle Group**

When designing your plan keep in mind how many sets per muscle group you need to achieve per week. Bigger muscle groups like: legs, chest and the back, need more sets per week to develop than smaller muscle groups like the biceps, triceps, shoulders, etc. Choose to do between 15 and 25 sets a week per bigger muscle groups and between 10 and 20 for smaller muscle groups.

Mass Gain/Bulk and The "Cut"

The mass gain phase is an important period when it is necessary to bring enough calories to the body to maintain a positive calorie balance, in order to minimize muscle catabolism and promote hypertrophy. This calorie load is necessary because of the amount of energy supplied to training! During a bulking phase your aim could be to put on some weight through increased calorie intake to increase your muscle gain.

During this caloric surplus period you will build a lot of muscle quickly but it is important to set off every so often so your body can recover from all the training and heavy eating. This process is called a "cut" and I recommend you do it twice a year. During the cut you will lose a bit of fat but keep most of your muscle. This period will let your digestive system and joints regenerate for the next mass gain. Without the cuts you will eventually stagnate and your progress will slow down.

Types Of Weekly Plans

I will now tell you the different kinds of weekly plans you can use to organize your work week. Choose the one that works the best for you and your needs. Remember to always start every training day with a warm up. After a good warm up you want to go ahead with practicing one of your core movements first as they are the most demanding so you will need the energy to execute them. Then add additional movements to add volume to your workout. Choose the rep range according to your needs and use the hypertrophy needs that I talked about earlier.

The Split
The most common training plan called the split consists of training each muscle part once a week usually to failure(till you can't go no more). The advantage of this plan is that it is simple to follow and easy to plan. It used to be the most common training plan used by most blokes in the gym but recent studies have shown that there are more efficient ways for both hypertrophy and strength.

One good trick to use when planning is to combine muscle groups that work together into one day to save time during your sessions e.g. train triceps together with the chest, as most chest exercises do work the triceps a little as well so you may as well finish it off with a few tricep sets.

Example of a split:

Monday: Chest + Triceps
1. Core movement - barbell bench press 4-5 sets
2. Incline dumbbell or barbell bench press 4 sets
3. 2 Additional chest exercises 4 sets each e.g. chest flies and push ups to finish off.
4. 3 additional exercises of 4 sets each for the triceps

Wednesday: Back + Biceps
1. Core movement - Barbell row 4-5 sets
2. 2nd core movement - Lat pulldown or pull ups 4 sets

3. 2 or 3 exercises of 4 sets each of additional back exercises like dumbbell rows and back machines.
4. 3 additional exercises of 4 sets each for the biceps.

Friday: Legs + Shoulders
1. Core movement - squat or deadlift 4-5 sets
2. 3 additional leg exercises 4 sets each e.g. front squat, lunges, leg extensions.
3. Core movement - barbell shoulder press 4 sets
4. 2 additional exercises 4 sets each e.g. dumbbell shoulder presses and lateral raises.

You can structure this plan differently to suit your needs e.g. do arms and shoulders on seperate days to workout 5 days a week.

Push-Pull Plan
This plan splits your workout into two parts. The push consists of the chest, shoulders and triceps. The pull muscles are the back and biceps. The legs can be combined with either push or the pull day or can be worked out on a seperate day, creating a push/pull/legs plan.

This plan is generally for more advanced lifters but can have great benefits as it's generally split into two parts meaning that if you train 4 times a week you can work each muscle group twice a week, which has a great advantage over the split. Doing that you will need to split your sets per week per muscle group into two and allocate for each of your training sessions.

Using this plan your muscles will be in hypertrophy almost the entire week as a beginner can regenerate for 72 hours after a workout. However, again you will need some experience before you can determine how to structure this plan.

Example of a Push-Pull - legs done on a pull day and only 2 sessions a week:

Monday: Push
1. Core movement - barbell bench press 4-5 sets
2. Incline dumbbell or barbell bench press 4 sets
3. Core movement - barbell shoulder press 4 sets
4. 2 Additional chest exercises 4 sets each e.g. chest flies and push ups to finish off.
5. 3 additional exercises of 4 sets each for the triceps
6. 2 additional exercises 4 sets each e.g. dumbbell shoulder presses and lateral raises.

Notice that the most demanding exercises are performed first and the additional exercises are done last.

Thursday: Pull
1. Core movement - use the deadlift to work both the legs and back
2. Core movement - Barbell row 4-5 sets
3. 2nd back core movement - Lat pulldown or pull ups 4 sets
4. 3 additional leg exercises 4 sets each e.g. front squat, lunges, leg extensions.
5. 2 or 3 exercises of 4 sets each of additional back exercises like dumbbell rows and back machines.
6. 3 additional exercises of 4 sets each for the biceps.

As you can see this plan can be a lot more demanding but there is more recovery time. However, there are more options with it as you can choose to workout 2 times a week if you are too busy to come into the gym 4 times a week.

You can still choose to workout 4 times a week to maximize hypertrophy. Again you will have to half the amount of sets you do in a workout and this plan would be very demanding.

Upper/Lower Body Plan
This plan is the most popular amongst professional bodybuilders. Again this plan is more advanced, splitting your body into two

parts: upper(chest, back, shoulder, triceps and biceps) and lower(quads, hamstrings, glutes, core and calves).

This plan can be similar to the push-pull plan, depending on how you structure the latter. With this plan it is easier to structure to workout 4 times a week twice on every muscle group. I don't need to supply you with an example as it would be similar as in the last plan example.

Additional Tips

As a beginner you will want to try different things out and see what works best for you and brings you the best progress. Therefore, don't be scared to adjust your training plan frequently and learn how to make it fit your own needs. Remember to use a training log to note all your lifts, so that you can revise your progress and adjust your plan accordingly.

HYPERTROPHY FINAL TIPS

We're getting close to the end of this book. I hope by now you have understood the basic principles of weightlifting and building muscle and are ready to hit the ground running with your first week of training. Before we finish however, here are a few golden nuggets for building muscle fast:

Tip No 1: A High Protein Meal In The Morning Helps You Gain Muscle

If you are looking above all for fairly simple bodybuilding advice, this one will please you; a hearty breakfast gives you the energy you need to last until your next meal. According to experts, you tend to eat healthier when your day begins with a balanced meal. Take pleasure in enjoying a delicious omelet in the morning to increase your muscle mass, and do not deprive yourself of cottage cheeses or smoothies. It is a very good idea to start your day with a high protein meal as it increases your muscle protein synthesis.

Tip No 2: Drink Lots Of Water

Heavy training causes water loss through sweating, which can interfere with recovery; and that may not increase your muscle mass. Drinking before going to the gym prevents dehydration and starvation, as an empty stomach can make you feel hungry. You can also take creatine monohydrate as a supplement. It is a source of energy that helps you train better.

Tip No 3: Eat At Set Times On Most Days

Respecting meal times is a crucial tip for a good bodybuilding process. According to the pros, you should eat breakfast, lunch, and dinner at the same frequency. By keeping your food intake high, you are not as hungry as when you have small dinettes more often. And by eating at set times every day, your body will now be hungry only at these times.

Tip No 4: Eating Protein With Every Meal Maximizes Protein Synthesis

To build muscle fast, you need to eat at least 1g of protein per 1kg of body weight, or more if you want. The easiest way to get this amount is to get a source of whole protein with each meal. Eating protein with every meal also means that your body will always be synthesizing protein for muscle mass.

Tip No 5: Perform Reasonable Workouts

It is always difficult to move forward when you are new to difficult exercises. So take it easy, because carrying heavy weights for the first workout does not boost muscle mass. This exhausts you more quickly and increases the risk of fatigue. Take it slow, lest you quickly get discouraged. Also take time to recover from exercise, and get at least 8 hours of sleep at night. It is essential for the health of your muscles.

Tip No 6: Don't Train Every Day

The pros recommend training for no more than 2 consecutive days and limiting exercise to 4 times a week. Even if you are your number one motivator, the desire to gain muscle doesn't have to dominate the rest of your life. Let each session bear fruit before starting the next. Also, carry out your workouts for a maximum of 90 minutes. According to scientists, your endogenous hormone levels drop dramatically after fifty minutes of hard work. Spending more time in sport can make you happy when you are not progressing.

Tip No 7: Adopt The Best Exercises

The pros do multi-joint exercises like squats, pull-ups, dips, bench press, etc... in particular, they involve several muscles at the same time. Do not try to do them on the same day to build muscle quickly. It is a gradual process. By performing one exercise after another, your body evolves and adapts to the heavier loads. This is when you can increase the weights. Also choose the exercises that work the best for you. Some exercises are great for building muscle, but if they're no good for you just scrap them.

Tip No 8: Don't Eat Before A Workout

You should allow at least 2 hours after your last meal before hitting a workout. Having food right before a workout will make it a lot harder for you to exercise because when you eat all of your blood goes down into your digestive tract to aid digestion and your body focuses most of its energy on digestion and little is left for the muscles. Furthermore, by working out right after eating you are confusing your body and crippling your digestion, decreasing the rate of absorption of your food.

Tip No 9: Use Lifting Accessories

Lifting belts, lifting straps, elbow and knee sleeves and fat grips are all amazing accessories I recommend you try out for your weight training. A lifting belt is the best accessory to consider as it can increase the weight you lift in compound exercises by about 5% and protect your lower back from injury. Lifting straps are great for deadlifts and sleeves are great for people with joint problems or for just additional safety. Fat grips are a great inexpensive accessory that will make your biceps grow faster.

CONCLUSION

Sports, in general, and weightlifting in particular have huge health benefits in teaching us body and mind discipline. And in weightlifting everyone can find the exercises that represent him or her.

One of the most important benefits of hypertrophy and physical exercise in general is that it not only helps you become fit, but also to gain a perfect shape. A moderate daily physical activity in addition to hypertrophy exercises; can even help prevent possible overweight and obesity. Taking into account the huge growth of obesity rate in the entire world, and especially the developing counties, making the practice of sports is an important and mandatory routine everyone shall start practicing.

This book has provided you with everything you need to know about hypertrophy, starting from its concept to its benefits, exercises and various elements that are related to hypertrophy in general. Besides, once you get the form you are looking for, this can help you find the inner peace you are looking for; it is somehow a way to relax although it can be tiresome at the beginning, but the result will pay off.

Training can also teach you that nothing is impossible; so you won't give up easily. I hope one of the most precious lessons this book will teach you is that training is an entire lifestyle and a new way of life that helps you overcome your everyday life challenges.

Always check your health before starting weightlifting and always make sure to choose the exercises that correspond to your own preferences and that go hand in hand with your fitness level.

Thank you for reading this book and I hope you have benefited from it!

BONUSES

Thank you very much for reading my book, I hope I have provided you with a plethora of useful information. Can I please ask you to leave your review of this book on Amazon to let others know what you think of it and help me update it in the future.

US review link

UK review link

I would like to provide you with an additional resource of information from which you can gather more training information, the website of my fitness brand Gainz Muscle Gear. (https://gainzmusclegear.com/)

My brand focuses on developing practical fitness products with cool branding.

My first product could be of high value to you.

Our Gainz Fat Grips will transform your arm workouts and accelerate your journey to big and strong arms! Please check this product out on my webpage.

Also visit our Facebook page

And our Instagram page.

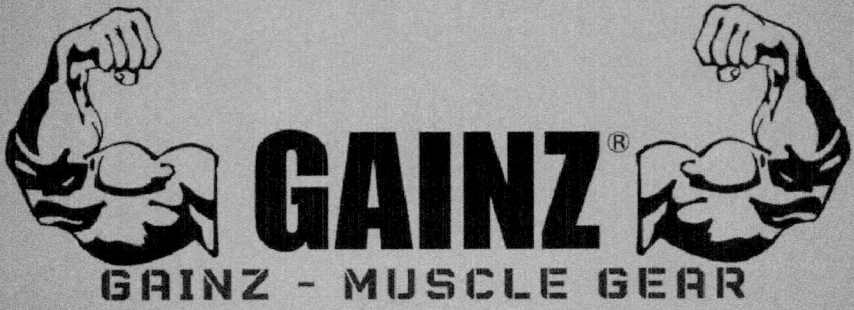

Printed in Great Britain
by Amazon